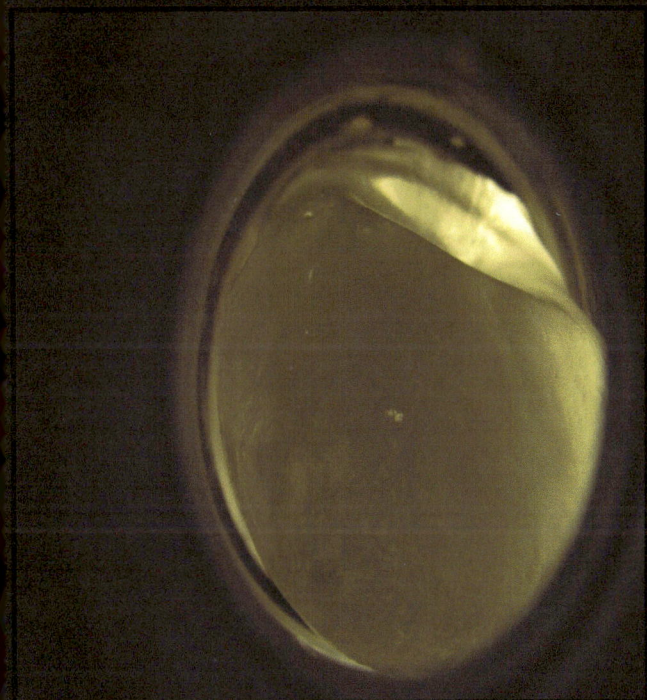
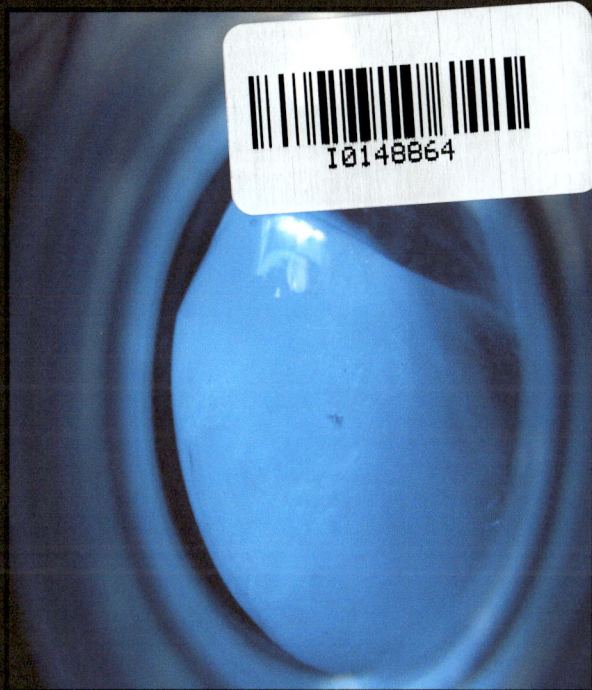

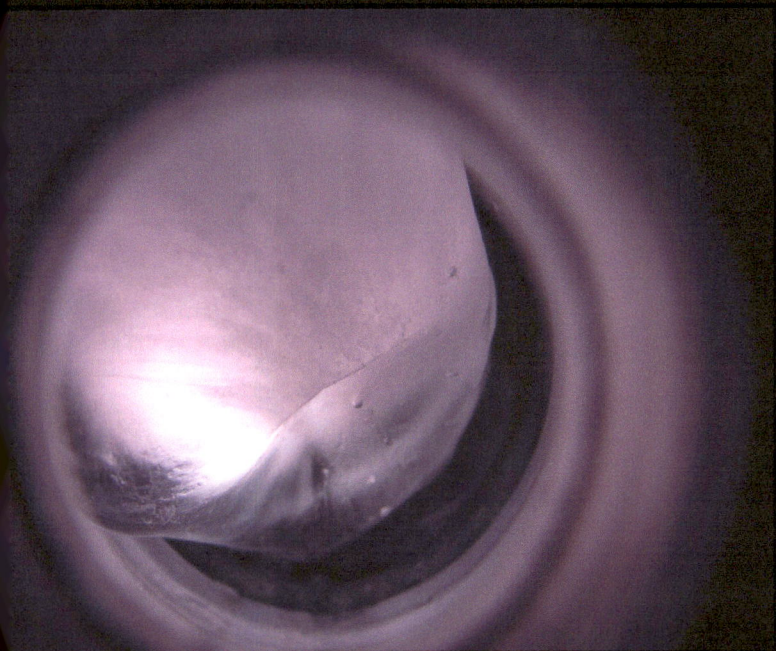
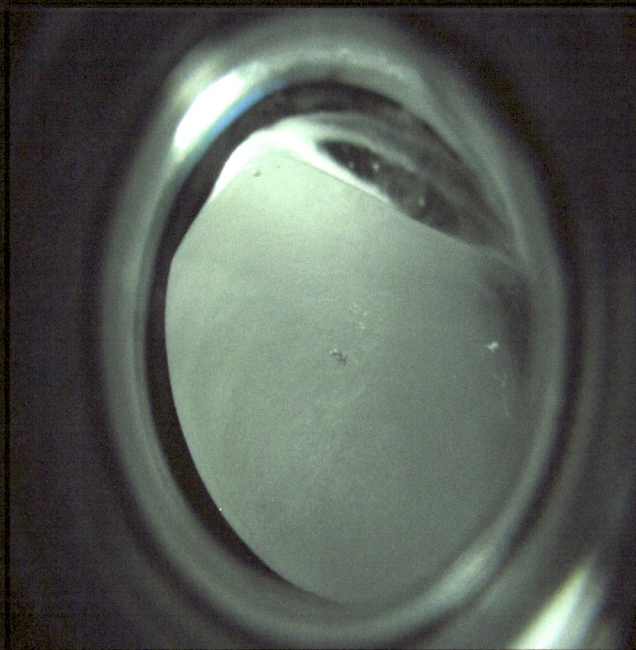

The Shorstors A Collection

of

Musings

By Tisha

Publishing, all creative literary content, photography, designs and editing
by: Tisha

Tisha, 1968- , The Shorstors A Collection of Musings by Tisha
Library of Congress cataloging in publication data
ISBN: 978-0-692-74354-6
10 9 8 7 6 5 4 3 2 1
1. Shortors/Short Stories 2. Poems & Prose 3. Quotes
4.Photography 5. Visual Art 6. Op-ed

(First Edition)

Soft cover edition 2016 printed in the U.S.A. by CreateSpace
Castellar, Monotype Corsiva ,Lucida Calligraphy & Magneto font types
Muscogee Creek Language; Mvto/thank you and Hesaketvmese/God
Canon Powershot S3 IS 6.0 mp

Special Thanks

to

Love...

~Contents~

~My Musings~

Prose, Poems, Quotes, Q-Ske's & Pics

~Presenting the Shorstors~

A Shorstor is a short story, a blending of words, that weave,
the tales of old,
into the tales of today; moving toward future lessons
for all generations, for all people,
with bright hopes...
This Collection of Shorstors are remnants of a life.
They are truths, fictions, fears, whimsies, musings and hope filled quest.
We have all lived during these times; as well as the spirits of our
Ancestors, which run deep.
Their Shorstors,
live within us; even though they have departed.
From the beginning of time, our ancestors have weaved a common bond.
Through their stories and journeys; some good, some bad. They have
helped us all
untangle life's difficulties along the way.
Within these stories
are the seeds of life; they are the tools for living.
We must never forget the moments together,
when we have shared
our fondest memories, with our loved ones, friends and confidantes...
For they contain our...

Shorstors.

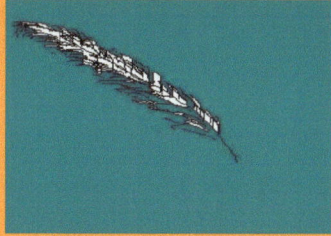

The Lessons of Little Chief

~prologue~

Many, many moons ago their was a young chief,
this he knew he would be;
from the time of the grasshoppers at his feet.
As the sun rose and the sun set, he dreamed
of tribal greatness. As he grew tall, the great ones
would tell him of his progress and his responsibilities.
He knew if he kept working hard at learning the
ways of his people, success would surely look
down on him. The elders thought much of his
growing potential and watched over him, in the
way of the Eagle.
Many moons later, the Little Chief had
a mission, that would normally be handled by a
more experienced chief. Full of pride, at the
quest and opportunity, the
Little Chief, tried to stay humble and fulfill his
duties and his destiny...

And so for Little Chief the lessons began...

Little Chief and the Lesson of the Great Ants

One day Little Chief and his father walked along the trail made many moons ago
by their ancestors. The worn grass and clay, molded like a sculpture by the
footprints of a long lost tribe, this they observed, while Little Chief and his father enjoyed
a beautiful spring day.
Little Chief, pointed out a multitude of things as usual, like the
bluish-violet sky, the white clouds with hues of gray and pink
and
the storm clouds in the distance.
He marveled at the opening yellow sunflowers which
bloomed every year in the same place, around the same time.

Little Chief and the Lesson of the Great Ants

He loved walking along this path and noticing the
great sacred pines,
he had seen, once,
twice
and more times than he could count.
Little Chief was always overwhelmed by his fathers teachings and tried to take
them in and remember them with all his might. His father seemed to think that he knew
a lot more than he did and told him at a pace
his little mind and little heart could not hold.
In spite of this, he tried and tried. So, one particular day. Little Chief's dad showed
him the "Great Ant" trails along the path. He told him that the ant's ancestors
had been there before them and probably shared the path with their own
great ancestors. They have lived a long life and their kind, has suffered greatly.
Their queens, decimated and their plight hardened by the actions of humanity.
They must survive as we do and their existence depends on working together
and
respecting those put in place to lead them.
Teamwork is their ultimate goal.

Little Chief and the Lesson of the Great Ants

It is their road to survival. Little Chief asked his father, how he
could help them?
The Chief told his son. "You respect them by understanding and
learning
what you can about their world and in the end, letting them live,
respectfully amongst nature."
The Big Chief exclaimed!, "It's how we all should live, it's what
I want and what our ancestor's wanted, it can be and hopefully
will be one day." Little Chief and his father,
watched the activities of the "Great Ant's", it seemed for hours.
Studying their great work ethic. One ant picking up a leaf
and
carrying it, another picking it up
after the other tired.
Another little sick ant seemingly
for whatever reason, did not make it
and went on the long journey. The other ant's scurrying nearby,
to come to its aid.

Little Chief and the Lesson of the Great Ants

Then a beautiful thing happened.
One ant begins to pull
the other ant.
It was a sight to see. Like fallen warriors.
One tried to pull the other,
to safety.
It appeared the poor little ant, was here
no more in spirit.
Little Chief watched in amazement, as so did his
father. Because even natures lesson's,
do not get old.
It was a beautiful day to learn and grow.
It was a beautiful day to be an ant; as well as, an
indigenous soul,
connected to nature.
Little Chief asked his dad if the ant's had
a happy life?

Little Chief and the Lesson of the Ants

The Big Chief, proclaimed, "Well my son, look at them.
They are many, abundantly providing for their group.
With strength in numbers they
produce what they need.
It seems maybe, like us,
this may be something that makes them
happy, or content."
Little Chief looked at the ant's again
and
then looked back at his dad and said.
"I think your right dad,
they seem happy."

Little Chief and the Lesson of the Ants

As they continued to walk along the trail, Little Chief kept
thinking about the ant's and thought of his own tribe
and
what they needed; to be just like the ants.
He thought that when he got back home, he would tell his friend's
about the lessons his dad had taught him and that he would
explain to them that if they stuck together, they too
could be a small,
but mighty tribe, built up of many little warriors,
showing teamwork, persistence, relentless work ethic,
strength and courage.
These things
Little Chief learned from walking on the trail that his ancestor's made,
before him, his father, or his father's father was born.
Many moons ago.

~The End~

Little Chief and the Lesson of Fishing

Little Chief's father came to
him one morning and said, "You are
old enough to learn how to fish in the ways
of the great warriors.
I want to teach you how to work with nature, to use
only
what you need for yourself and your tribe.
To show respect to our ancestors
and
to the many life forms that help us to survive.
Son it is about respect, not
just hunting and not just
to eat. Our intent is to honor all of what we use
And
To use all remains.
It is not our intention to do harm.
We made a pact, to give and take. Sometimes, we must take,
but with respect.
Sometimes we must give and again with respect.
It is the law of the land and of our ancestors,
who came before us
and
who taught us these ways, for our survival."

Little Chief and the Lesson of Fishing

"We must love all things and treat them as if
we are all connected, even in death,
we must always show respect."
Little Chief listened and thought deeply about what his
father told him.
What a great father he had, so strong so smart, so kind.
He looked forward to his lesson.
Little Chief and his father
walked along the trail near
the old fishing pond, fished by
seven generations of indigenous peoples of all tribes, as well as
many other's from faraway lands.
It was the place where youthful lessons became;
the warrior stories of the
elders.

Little Chief and the Lesson of Fishing

It was the place where the
lesson of hunting
and
living off the land became clear.
Little Chief's father said, "Before we begin,
we will pray for a good bounty and for the fish to bless our clan,
by sharing their great honor with us."
We will honor the
sacred pact that our ancestors
made before us and show respect and let them know
we will abide by our forefather's agreements, to take and give back,
when our time shall come. In turn we will share our bounties
with their generations and in this we all survive, in
the spirit of connectedness.
The Big Chief, brought out his blessing pouch, filled with
Cedar,
White sage
and
Tobacco.

Little Chief and the Lesson of Fishing

He spread the white sage amongst the trees,
where they stood, sprinkled some in the water and blessed the
whole of things, such as: the hand-woven oak basket, my Mom made us
for good luck. Made from the trees on our land.
My father even blessed
the worms and thanked them for their
sacrifice and gift to our family.
These are the very spirits in nature that
our own ancestor's had made a pact with long, long ago.
The Big Chief then told his son, "We will fish now."
Little Chief's father then took out
his fishing pole and slowly
untangled the line and hook,
showing Little Chief how to unhook it safely from the pole.
He then unlatched the
basket, which contained all the
essential tools for a good and respectful day of fishing.
This my father did in silence.

Little Chief and the Lesson of Fishing

Little Chief's father then put the little worm on the hook.
As he put the line in the water,
he silently
admired nature's beauty
and
lifted his strong indigenous face to the wind
and
the sky.
Little Chief watched every move his father made,
taking special care to remember the blessings
as
Little Chief, seemed especially sensitive to these types of things.
He wondered how long it would be
and
if they would be blessed with a fish.

Little Chief and the Lesson of Fishing

He learned that in respect to nature peacefulness was needed.
They did not sing, chant, or laugh.
The elders in the tribe knew this of him
and
it is why he was selected at a young age for the special teachings, by
the Chiefs.
Little Chief watched as the waves in the water moved the line back
and
forth.
Little Chief's father told him beforehand,
that it
was not a prideful moment, not an act of competition,
but a task of survival and trust.
Little Chief found himself staring at the line,
waiting for that distinct, tug or
downward movement of the line,
his elders talked
about in their many nights around the
storytelling circle.

Little Chief and the lesson of Fishing

His father described it to him, but with the
water
moving so much, he did not quite
understand.
He than began to feel sleepy.
Little Chief whispered to his dad. "Should we pray again?"
His dad held up his hand, as if to gesture, silence.
The sun beamed bright and bird's
made their presence known.
Squirrels, Eagle hawks, Ravens, Cottontail deer
and Beavers all made their homes,
near the old fishing pond.
The wind blew
and
the trees swayed as Little Chief fought and fought against sleep.
He could not see how his father did it.
He looked at his father again
and
wondered if he would grow up to look like his father,
one day.

Little Chief and the lesson of Fishing

He picked
a spot on the water to stare at
and
watched the rippled designs come and go.
The Big Chief then looked at his son,
restless and young.
He then whispered to him, "Patience Little Chief."
It was at that moment, in which a downward movement
occurred and the water began to move, like
Little Chief had not seen before. His eyes glazed in excitement,
almost letting out a yell, but it was a restrained silent yell,
as quiet and patience were a part of today's lesson.
Little Chief did not expect to feel the way he did, considering
a few moments prior;
he was falling asleep.
He had started to think of fishing as a boring thing to do, that
he was not
looking forward to.

Little Chief and the Lesson of Fishing

The tug grew more
and
more distinct
and
The Big Chief remained calm.
He slowly rose from his seating position
and
with perseverance,
began to reel in the line. He pulled in the string, little by little
and
the
beautiful fish emerged from the water.
The fish in all its beauty was the length of my father's hand
two times.
It twinkled in the sun, with many colors of the rainbow.

Little Chief and the Lesson of Fishing

My father a man of about thirty moons,
smiled and lifted the fish up in the air.
He flipped and flopped around
and
twisted and tried to get a way. It seemed my father
and
him
may have been equals. But,
someone would have to sacrifice
for the good of all.
In our area, the elder's often spoke of
Salmon, Rainbow Trout, Perch and Bass.
My dad began another prayer. He thanked the
Creator
for the fish
And for health and abilities to fish for his tribe, he asked for the spirit of
the fish to be at peace and thanked the fish for it's
abundance and nourishment.
The fish seemed to calm in its movements.
Little Chief imagined the fish receiving a high honor in the fish world.

Little Chief and the Lesson of Fishing

The Big Chief
then took the fish off the hook,
with care and mercy.
I watched patiently and with a continued sadness.
Little Chief did not fully understand this part yet.
In the stories of the elders the fish had sacrificed his
life, leaving his family and friends,
the freedom to swim in the waters, to see the sky
and
to have life, for us?!
It was hard to believe. Would the Big Chief do this?
Would Little Chief?
This was definitely a lesson that would have to
be explained more to me.
Little Chief felt the
tears
welling up as the fish struggled
for its last breath of this life.
Little Chief began to cry.

Little Chief and the Lesson of Fishing

My father then looked at me with his strong and gentle
eyes, as if he understood exactly what I was feeling. He then said,
"Little Chief, it is good you feel the sadness of your heart.
It is the mark of a great Chief and warrior, for the people;
"If you feel these things you will remember respect
and
kindness to nature.
You will learn not to take more than you need
and you will be grateful for nature and its
abundant gifts.
"A great man you will be one day,
if you follow these lessons, my son."
I wiped my tears from my face
and watched my father take the fish and place
it in the woven basket. He then took
sage and spread it over the basket and finally my
Father smoked a little tobacco near the area where we sat all day.
My father was giving a final reverence
to the fish and it's ancestors.
We then gathered our belongings
and journeyed back on the trail to our home.
Walking the path of our ancestor's,
yesterday, today and
tomorrow.

~The End~

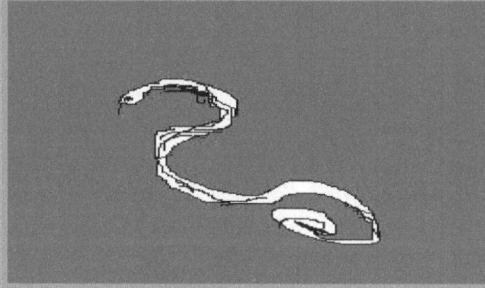

Little Chief and the Lesson of the Snake

One day Little Chief's father and Uncle sat him down.
His teachings of the tribes history,
were about to commence.
Although Little Chief felt very confident and sure of himself,
even at a very early age; He grew nervous
and
concerned about his abilities and strived not to let his elders down.
This day his father told him of the story of
his brother who went out unto the
world for an education at
A traditional University.

Little Chief and the Lesson of the Snake

The family although very proud of him,
was concerned that he would learn the ways of the world
and
forget about the old ways of the indigenous peoples.
My uncle was home on break and while
spending time with the family, in communion with the land.
He was bitten by a snake and took the long journey home.
All his wisdom in the new world,
did not prepare him for this and he had forgotten the
wisdom of the land,
such as: How to walk with a stick on the land,
for this will help you to move leaves, smaller
sticks and mounds
of dirt and rocks in your
path.

Little Chief and the Lesson of the Snake

Watch out for the spit of the snake, it looks
like soap suds on top of the grass, also look out
for snake holes.
Sometimes, it's hard to know the difference between
a
gopher hole and a snake hole,
but both should be left alone and in peace.
Also, all creatures are connected to us in a
brother/sisterhood.
They are
sacred
and
our intent is not to harm
and in turn, we hope that
they will not harm us.

Little Chief and the Lesson of the Snake

Unfortunately,
my youth
does not let me know all things.
They will have to come with time.
In our culture the snake is a sacred animal of
wisdom and a protector of the
Medicine Men/Women.
After my father told me this story;
I could not help but
wonder why the snake hurt my uncle, did he do something wrong?
These questions made me restless.
My father said that a sharing of
wisdom
was gained and the snake brought snake medicine to us.
Although we lost a loved one,
we gained a better understanding of the world around us,
we gained experience.

Little Chief and the Lesson of the Snake

Some Medicine Men/Women know how
to save a person from a poisonous snake bite.
However, these techniques are very old and set aside
for certain natives, that are passed down, generationally.
If the snake did not direct us to its wisdom by its bite,
our people
would not have survived for so many generations.
Even though I expressed to my father that it kind of made sense to me.
Why could he not be saved and learn as well?
Many seasons ago our ancestor's made a pact
with the animals great and small
that we would respect each other
and
share our world.

Little Chief and the Lesson of the Snake

As we take the life of an animal, we pledge to respect
the sacred gift
and
in turn, when we return to the earth,
they accept our gift to them.
In this way, it is a type of recycling of life.
I asked my father, "So does this mean, when I die,
I will go to the snake's family?"
He laughed and said, "Little Chief,
you will return to the land of your ancestor's,
the land that has given to your people, yes you
will return to the earth,
to give back." He said,
"Be kind to all things and the
Master of Breath will be kind to you."
As the day ended, I thought about the teaching
and
grew thankful of a greater understanding of
my ancestor's, the world around us and what
my place was in it.

~The End~

The Butterfly and the Bee

One beautiful fall day a butterfly just happened
to flutter onto the same flower blossom, as a bee.
They greeted each other as all pollinators do,
with a flick of their antennas and a joyful hello.
"How are you, my friend?" The butterfly said. "
Well, I suppose." The bee said.
"What's wrong?" said the butterfly and so it began,
the bee started ruminating
about why it's so hard to be a bee.
"No one likes me!" The bee said.
"Well that's not true, why do you say that? Said the butterfly.
"It's because people are always swatting
at me and running away,
I'm just a little bee and
they are so much bigger
and
They are swatting at me;
can you
imagine?!"

The Butterfly and the Bee

"Why don't humans understand,
I'm just trying to do my job and it's very Important."
"I've got so much work to do, pollinating here and there,
and
if I don't finish my rounds; I don't know what will happen?!"
"Argh!"said the bee.
"Oh little bee, it happens to me too!"
"Oh come on, they love you, you're so pretty,
some say beautiful!
They look at you in awe and they do not fear you, like me."
said the bee.
The bee looked sad and the butterfly said, little bee,
"Maybe you shouldn't
sting them." The bee said,
"Well what am I supposed to do, someone nearly
sent me to
bee heaven
yesterday,

The Butterfly and the Bee

it's my only defense and I get so mad!"
"I know just how you feel, sometimes I have to
dodge cars and people,
it's hard to be small,
but some are smaller than us; your
little sting is mighty and some people are allergic
and
it can have devastating affects; that's why
some people are scared of you."
"Little bee, you can fly so
wonderfully
in order to get out of the way,
you should try that;
instead of
stinging;
Just keep focused on your task
and
I'm sure it will get better."
said the butterfly.
"Well ok, butterfly, you make sense to me
and guess what,

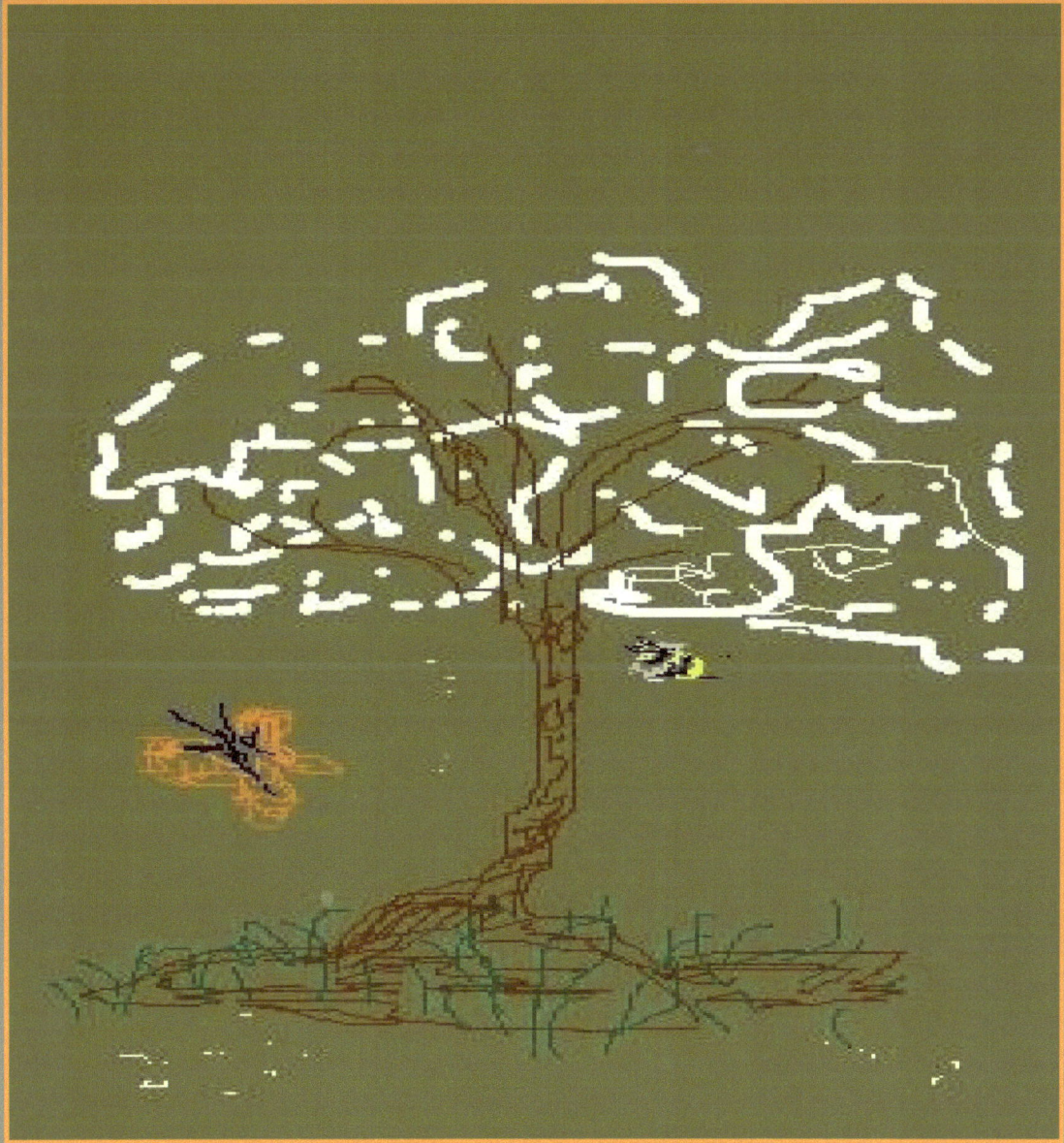

The Butterfly and the Bee

Today, was better,
a group of artist's
noticed us doing our job,
I hope we made them proud
and showed them, we can all get along.
It was nice to be admired,
so I suppose
Things are looking up!"
said the bee.
"Well, I must be on my way to join the flock in
South America,
they are expecting
me soon!

The Butterfly and the Bee

I had a delay,
because of a slight tumble with a passerby;
I hit her shoulder,
but thank goodness
she had a beautiful spirit and soul,
so it was worth it."
said the butterfly.
"Ok, hope to see you again one day
and
thank you so much for the advice."
Have a safe journey!
They both proclaimed and suddenly,
they both
flew away.

~The End~

The Leak Summit

A puddled mess accumulated on the floor; a
2 X 5
square inch radius,
almost completely covered by a substance.
What is it we wondered?
Where on earth did it come from? Is it from the unit upstairs?
Did the kitty have and accident?
Possibly a sewer back up or leak?
What?!
Upon further inspection it appeared to be coming from the ceiling.
Drip one, drip two fell and then more drips.
Drip, drip, drip!
We grabbed a bucket, mop and paper towels.
We argued, we consoled, we admonished, we debated
and
we planned.

The Leak Summit

We said how each other's ideas were
more impossible than the next,
we panicked,
we tried the farfetched ideas that were more
ridiculous
than the next, and
we failed, with all of them.
We kept trying and then we called the
building management.
An unlikely cast of characters,
that appeared to help us,
coordinate our fixes.
We left an urgent message, that the unit above us
appeared to be experiencing a leak,
from an unknown source.
Of course, this was on a Saturday afternoon, no answer,
no help,
until
Monday.

The Leak Summit

We were on our own.
We thought of plans to notify the tenant upstairs.
We then wrote a note to our good neighbors above, it read;
'Dear Neighbor, I am writing to let you know that
there appears to be some sort of leak coming from your unit.
I have notified the management company,
Thank you. Sincerely,
your Neighbor.'

The Leak Summit

Of course, we felt
uncomfortable leaving a note on the door,
as we went back to the task of
straightening out the bathroom debacle.
We waited on word from upstairs; to decide the
unsettling decision of who would interact
with our upstairs neighbor.
We had after all, summoned our guest.
Suddenly, just as our blood pressures began to reach a
recommended healthy state.
A tap at the door.
We looked at each other and then opened the door
and
their stood a stranger,
not the usual neighbor, but another
person.

The Leak Summit

We all introduced ourselves with the normal etiquette,
except that the neighbor shook hands twice and for some reason,
I thought it odd.
We explained the plight, again and he stated that he did not
observe any leaks upstairs.
However, on move in maybe
unclogging the tub may have caused some type of issue in the pipe.
Our neighbor than asked to come in and look at it.
At which time, we declined the entrance,
stating that we did not know of anyone new living up stairs
and
that they were a new tenant. The new neighbor stated, that they had only
just moved in a few days ago; and as we concluded the cross interrogation,
he proceeded to the
upstairs apartment and we our domain.
"No leaks, sorry I did not find any leaks."
It seemed the
Drip,
had subsided for now.
The interactions again made me think and get a little uncomfortable.
Why?
I was not sure.

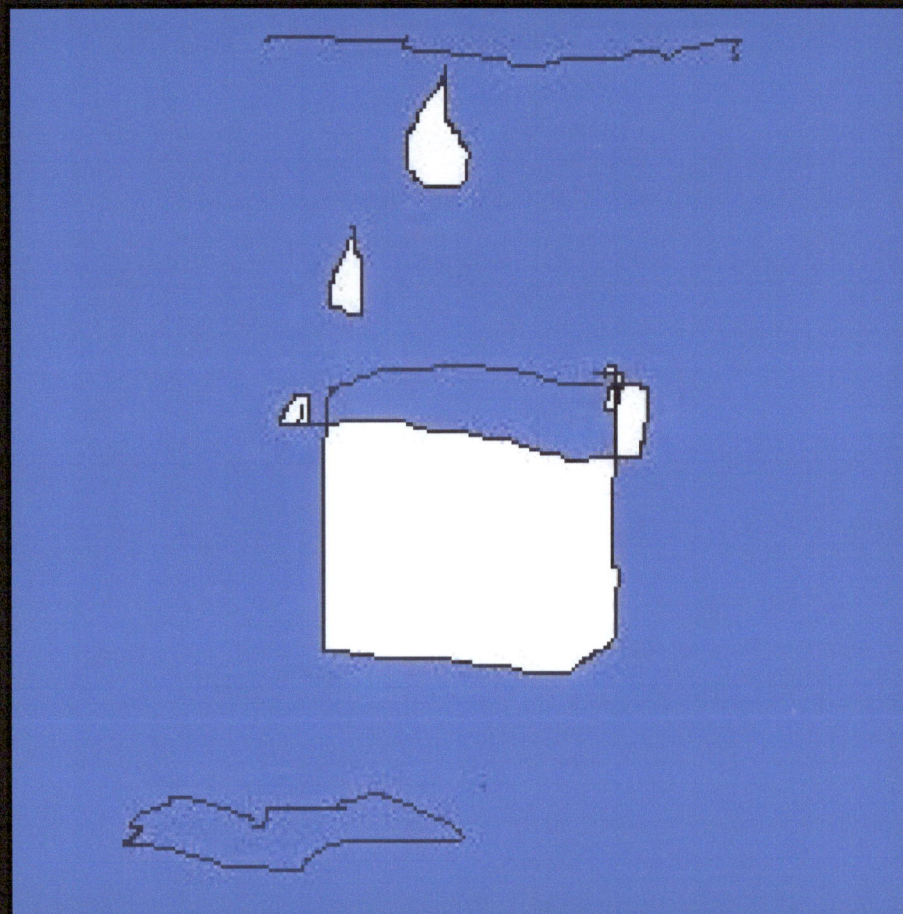

The Leak Summit

Monday,
was a new day and a close eye was kept on the
ceiling for leaks
and
creepy occurrences.
It stilled bothered me that this new person upstairs, still
appeared to have have no items of identity, with them.
I decided to go to the local convenience store, for a few items.
As I entered the store, I noticed a police officer,
finishing up his
coffee fusion,
getting it just right.
As he moved from the area, I began
to fill up my basket.
Then I noticed our new neighbor enter the store. I glanced
and
continued on my way, gathering my supplies.
The neighbor walked up
to the counter looked back at me, as if a
moment of recognition had occurred,
from the day before; then grabbed
something else from the
coffee
area and proceeded back to the checkout.

The Leak Summit

We acted as
if we had no prior
interaction from the day before.
Later my mind began to replay,
and
I remembered a horrible
experience I had some years before,
with a possibly, mentally ill person.
Something did not seem right. I also remembered about
two weeks ago a disturbance
or scratching at the door, I did not answer.
But, looked through the peep hole and it was this same person,
it was our new neighbor.
That day, the person turned away from the door
and
I only saw the back of their head.
A rogue person from my past left me with an
undiagnosed bought of
Post traumatic stress disillusion/disorder.

The Leak Summit

This person was triggering my symptoms.
I had heard somewhere
that the person had moved to
another state and the plates on this persons vehicle;
where from that same state.
Could this person be connected?
Yes, it seems that in these days
to nice is more suspect
than not being so nice.
My heart
started to beat faster and my mind raced at the thought
that somehow, this new tenant
was an accomplice;
living in our building.
Had they manipulated the
upstairs neighbor out of the apartment?

The Leak Summit

It was all a plot to get into our apartment.
Did they overflow their bathtub on
purpose to try to have a reason to come in to our
unit, or was it done to irritate us?
Where they thieves? Con artists?
Or maybe, just new neighbors meaning no harm,
an accidental calamity.
My mind was clearly up to it's old tricks.
The leak finally ceased and
the sound of footsteps above our heads persisted,
stomp, stomp and more stomp.
Time will tell,
as we wait for the next move,
or
the next
drip.

~Finito~

Windows of the Heart

Sallyann peered through the
window in awe and wonderment.
The Indian paintbrushes were
particularly
stunning that day
and
she was
astonished at the way they
had grown in such a short time.
Sallyann's heart was full and she just knew
she would be a butterfly one day,
she just knew it!
Mae, Sallyann's friend,
also looked out the window,
but quite a
different world
appeared to her.
She had no need for such things in her world.

Windows of the Heart

She wanted
Money and lots of it, to pay down all her bills
and
to buy all the things that she wanted.
She scoffed at
Sallyann's happiness and naivety,
as their
priorities
seemed quite different.
Somewhere
two different paths converged,
as well as two different views of life.
One of beauty, nature, love and joy
and
the other; consisting of wants,
power and greed.
Only time will tell, which window will be open.

~The End~

~ Musings~

Prose, Poems & Quotes

Each artist has
a view of red, yellow, blue.
However, chemical changes
within our brains,
dna and nervous
systems; alter the
multiple variations of colors
that emerge. Giving each
artist a unique and
finite color palette,
of which each
work of art is produced.
Specifically modeled
by the things that, take our breath away
and
illuminate us.
They are the things that

Move us.

In short...
Our Musings...

~Poem~

(It Isn't)
It isn't the sound of her voice when she cries.
It isn't the rage in her eyes, or the lies.
It isn't the moving tone of her gloat.
It isn't the grasping scream in her throat.
It isn't the phone ringing, per chance.
It isn't the fiery aggression, or stance.
It isn't the loss of mankind I fear.

It is the loss of hope,
That draws near.

~Prose~

(Oh how I miss Winter)

I miss Winter, can you believe it.
It is a first ever occurrence.
The silence, the slow pace,
the bitter cold, that kept all in, the wind that took our breaths away.
I miss Winter.
The perfect antidote to a bustling, loud, noisy, chaotic city.
The perfect vortex
Winter has left us and so it was.
Glistening ice crystals, gone to soon.
Birds flying in the midst, silence and stillness,
of
which we all needed to calm our souls.
Yes, bears must forage for food sometimes and sleep sometimes,
but oh the days of
two people
roaming around, my two made
four.

~Prose~

(Oh how I miss Winter, cont'd)

One below and wind chills thirty below,
Oh how I miss Winter, can you believe it?!
I am saddened, even though I have seen the green shoots
popping out, even though I have seen the pink forget me knots,
not forgetting,
even though the Cardinals song echo's in the wind.
The people, the people are everywhere and earlier than usual.
The masses, already beckon their bodies to the sun.
It is not the realm of introverts,
for the extroverts celebrate the coming of the circus.
Oh...how I miss
Winter,
can you believe it?!

~Poem~

(I Hear the Drums)

I hear the drums around me,
as an echo in my mind.
The soundtrack of a native beat,
that's older than mankind.
The whipping winds amongst us,
they blend with every beat.
The drums they are around me,
they hinder my retreat.
An artist has a calling,
of
which the drums call out.
A simple beat of rhythmic sound,
can guide... the soul... towards life... Profound...
The drums are calling me today.
My ancestors guide
the
drums that play.

~Poem~

(Love came to me I)

When you least expect the sun, it shines...
For love came to me, in the knick of time...
For my heart has been broken and time will tell...
In the midst of my healing you've cast a spell...
For it wasn't a planning, of things, you see...
It's just so happened that
love came to me...

~poem~

(If We Could Change the World)

I fell apart today, after realizing that tomorrow was far away.
These things my mind does tell, don't suite me very well.
The meanness in their hearts, break down my every part.
The crimes of men exist, far from their righteousness.
If we, If we could change the world.
Life lives us very well, but we have life's that fail.
We try them every time, searching blindly for the lines.
Forgetting who we are,
wounded with battle scars.
In little bitty ways, we make it through the haze.
If we, If we could change the world,
If we,
If we could
change
the
world.

(The Quotes)

My best friend is a rainbow. *-Tisha*

Rainbows don't lie. *-Tisha*

Solidarity only works when the base metals are solid. *-Tisha*

When niceties get you nowhere and cruelties get you everywhere,
there is nowhere to go. *-Tisha*

Love fractures, then heals. *-Tisha*

For love is not always gentile and kind,
it is at times
harsh and cruel.
It is in these times, we must
breathe and try again.
For every heartbeat is a
chance for redemption. *-Tisha*

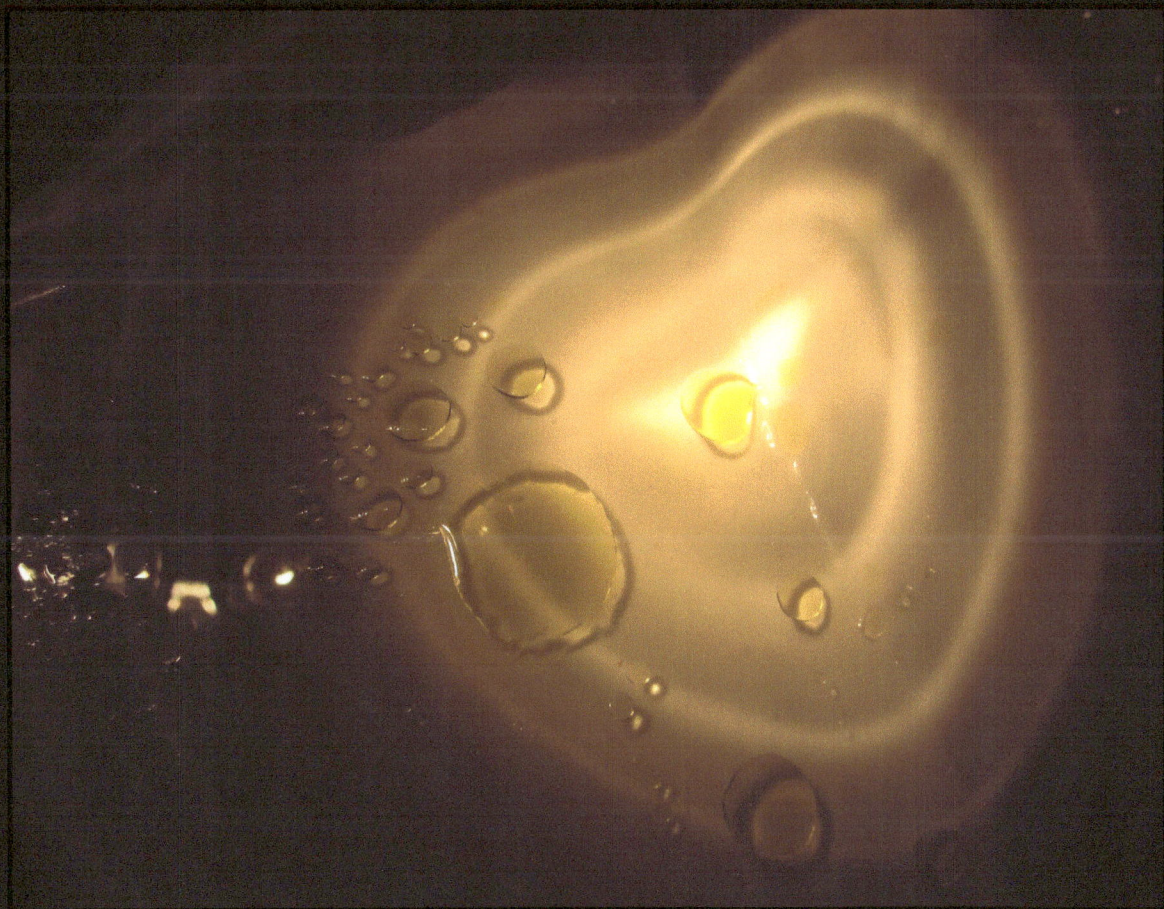

(Prose of the Heart)

Such misery abounds the closest hearts.
Family trials are many
and
retreat has failed.
Happy hearts fall into despair, my eyes sorrow,
but do not want to.
For these words are true, they are conscious.
My love of life transcends and evil leaves.
Let not the
troubled hearted
hold you back.
Their sorrows are many and mine,
lessened by the light, shortened by the days,
lifted to a higher place.
Do not fear for them,
for they will find guidance in your strength.
Your character shines and your heart is good.
Let not souls blur your eyes.
Become your
greatness.

~prose~

(To live in the time of the dragonflies)

One day our time will be no more,
From this earth we will exit.
But...
how wonderful it is, to live...
In the time of the
dragonflies,
the buzz of airplanes overhead, the whimsical swirls of clouds,
the misty rainy days,
the trees and sunflowers bent to the left and blooming,
graciously bowing, bravo, bravo.
The grass... green and full of life of a billion in it's soil.
It's called living...
Tasting ripened Mulberries, falling from trees like rain,
covering the ground, inch, by inch, mile by mile,
cut down in it's prime of life.
Living amongst it all the
festivals of
summer,
the artist with their wares in tow,
exuberant to display their art,
as well as begrudged.

~prose~

(To live in the time of the dragonflies, cont'd)

Shy and buoyantly
happy about the prospects of
communicating
the uncommunicative.
Colors, sounds, heartbeats jump out and say,
we are here.
and we want to love you, now...
Our earth is better for it, our minds are better for it,
our spirits are at peace and
happily breached.
We will not surrender
these golden opportunities to thrive and be alive.
One day our time will be no more.
But...Today my heart knows that
our souls
and
our energies combine moments that
will live on.
In the essence of all things simple and complex
Forevermore...
We lived in the time of the dragonflies.

~prose~

(I/WE have lived)

I/WE have loved and laughed.
I/WE have seen rainbows, sunrises and sunsets and painted them as well.
I/WE have felt joy and pain.
I/WE are not scared of death.
For what more could I/WE ask for.
I/WE have wanted and received our needs and needed and received our wants.
I/WE have smelled the roses.
I/WE have eaten beautiful food from all over the world and tasted the
wonderful montalcinos and chocolates.
Last but not least, my love affair with coffee, etc.
has not ceased, since my seventh birthday,
my beautiful sips and lips, remembered...

I/WE have lived.

~prose~

(Sequence)

In the quest for the power of the pen, I write,
Knowing absolutely nothing...
With wisdom unbound and uncharted,
It is my destiny to proclaim, all there is and what is known.
For if feeble minds know not, here is the story of humanity.
We are not, have not, from knots,
into knots;
simply two, simple four,
we are.
One,
we shall stand.
In us are many.
Toothless beginnings, toothless beggars and toothless endings.
On earth, the oceans,
the solar galaxies await our visits.
So this resolves our quest,
Ignited and subscribed on this day,
peace
To all human kind.

~poem~

(White Leaves)

The melody's of Winter sing out.
The beauty, the fall of Winter appears and it seems
like autumn, but only with
white leaves.
One by one the flakes pile on, they are I tell you white leaves.
As beautiful as any fall display of colors.
Without the vibrancy of a rainbow, but with a steely strength.
We are here, we compete, we are the leaves of Winter.

~poem~

(The Soul of Nature Whispers)

The soul of nature whispers, quietly at our ears.
Listen...
Listen...for your heart will wipe it's tears.
The soul of nature whispers,
for all of us that hear.
Share love and peace...
In your steps,
all of your days...
Hold onto life so tightly...
that you absorb it's
healing ways.
and
may you find yourself, within natures loving rays.

YESTERDAY'S COMMENTS
(A humble thought inspired by our fellow poster)
A fellow poster put up an image that stated "Be Who You Are" or something to that affect.
I observed a comment underneath that said. Does that mean even (ah's). In response
to this posting, I 1+1'd, as I could not post a comment to this group, as I'm not a follower of it.
Well it posed a question in my mind, of the statements of others: "keep it real" and
"born this way". So, here goes, if we know and understand that some people are truly born, with
mental disorders, developmental issues, compounded with the normal, daily anxieties and the
stressors of life. If we truly understand that we are all here to help each other get through the
tough times. If we ask all and we want all to keep it real, be human, be sincere and we under-
stand that "pain" has done this to us all, than we must allow for some to be who they are.

Except that they may be born this way. Except that they are keeping it real for themselves and
their capabilities, except that they are trying to desperately fit into a world that has said, this
is how we want you, without respecting,
"Be who you are". We are all guilty of bending and
being bent, however, we must try to love one another. In the cases of (ah's) as the post comment-
er said. Yes, even (ah's), we should love them and understand, that our world, our cultures, or
belief systems and our failures have contributed to all the wrongs and rights against humanity.
We are one world, one heart, one soul, one spirit. If we in effect, those of us, who know how to
love;
without
hurting one another.
Teach the ones who don't, we may have a chance. We must have compassion and honest justice
for the difficult cases. If we only believe, (WE) can make a difference;
It's up to us all.
Finally, to the (ah's) we love you, but do not always like your particular way of functioning in
this world. However, we are all shaped into what we have become. You most likely feel the
same about us. Us meaning, the days we aren't being an (ah). Underneath our difficulties we
must always
LOVE ONE ANOTHER;
it's the only true shield we have.

(Quotes)

Forever may I
reach the boundaries of my heart
the stars will guide me. -Tisha

Plans
are for people who
believe
in the illusion of control. -Tisha

Flowers bloom somewhere
the sun is full of visions
we all love the sun. -Tisha

Water is conscious
for we are unconscious life
striving for water. -Tisha

~To:
Our love
is
beyond
Immortal Explanations
be with me...
my love...
~From:

(Quotes)

The ant lives its' life
through persistence and teamwork.
Ant's give gravity.-*Tisha*

We must not fear...
We must hope...
We must not care, less...
We must care, more...
We can not have to many "I's"
We must have we's and ours and togetherness...
All of us...-*Tisha*

~665 poem 665~

No way out of this... but into you...
My heart weeps for the unknown...
For you are the uncertainty principle...
In form and shape.

[Quotes]

Forever Love Can.-Tisha

Sentimentalities persist in our minds.
For all time, there are the memories.
We must gasp a breath of hope,
when faith leaves us and remember
our pulse. -Tisha

Our allies become our enemies
and
our enemies become our allies.
Within all of us lies eminent love,
we must find it every moment,
of every day.
Within every human there is hope,
that can be found. -Tisha

[Quotes]

There are no easy answers to life,
but there are easy questions.
Within the questions are the answers.
How do we end poverty?
End poverty.
How do we end war?
End War.
How do we love one another?
Love one another.
It's that simple!
We must begin today. *-Tisha*

Happiness said hello to me today
and
I said hello my friend
and
may you have a long life. *-Tisha*

I love you...
In time and space...
In places we don't know of yet.... *-Tisha*

With special thanks to
Hesaketvmese/The Creator...

To all my ancestors, loved ones
and
beautiful souls...ᴍʀ who have
journeyed the trails
with me, each day to fulfill our destinies,
our loves & our musings. Thank you.
May we continue to make our
dreams come true.

To all the living and spirit beings that allowed their
images to be captured. From my fulfilled heart, thank you...

Mvto/Thank you, for your valuable time with me...

Love you all... Infinitely,
Tisha

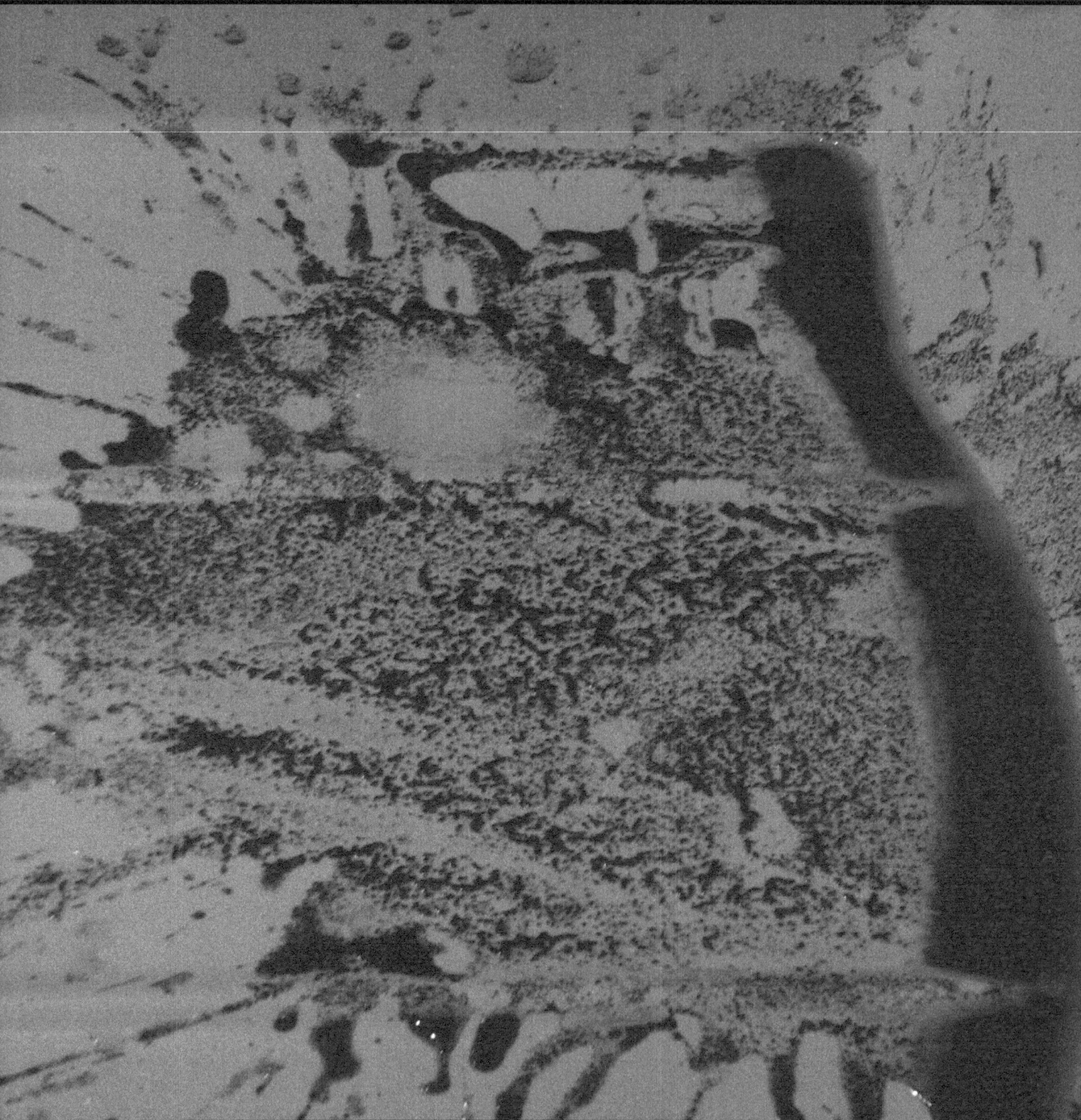

Love One Another - *Jesus*

In Loving Memory of Beloved Piccolo

www.ingramcontent.com/pod-product-compliance
Lightning Source LLC
Chambersburg PA
CBHW042005080426
42733CB00003B/19